Riding the Moments:

The whirl within ... !!!

Seema Singh

BookLeaf Publishing

India | USA | UK

Dedication

To each and every life that triggered me to pen this book, and to the readers who will pick it up and breathe life into its words, sentences, and ideas— bringing meaning to the moments captured within these pages.

Acknowledgement

I would like to express my heartfelt gratitude to the Editor and support team of BookLeaf Publishing for providing me with the platform and opportunity to showcase my penned emotions and ideas, inspired by various moments and situations that caught my fancy. I am especially thankful for the challenge they presented, which I accepted and, in doing so,proved my mettle and tenacity of purpose to myself.

In Montreal, Canada, I am deeply grateful to my dear daughter, Srjanaa, my dear son-in-law, Sagar, and my dearest, dearest "lighthouse" grandson. Together, you are the anchors of my life and the very essence of my world.

In Delhi, I extend my heartfelt thanks to my husband, Dr. B.I. Fozdar, for always standing by my side, offering unwavering support, and giving me the space and time to nurture my creative expression.

In Pune, I am immensely thankful to my son, Kaustubh S. Fouzdar, who serves as a perpetual lighthouse of motivation for me.

Lastly, I am profoundly grateful to my parents, my extended family members and my friends for their love and encouragement throughout my journey.

Preface

"I divide all literary works into two categories: those I like and those that I don't like. No other criterion exists for me."

—Anton Chekov

Writing with the above underpinnings is easy. Simultaneously, expressing one's ideas and thoughts for readers' consumption is important, for only then does the expression becomes alive and relevant. Being an ardent and avid observer of nature and factoring experiences into my consciousness has been a placid pastime for me before I felt the urge to document it. This urge, over a period of time, took the shape of a diary—a coveted confidant! At first, it was small ideas spun into phrases; small snippets, minute observations, and insights, and so on. I collected them like pebbles from a flowing river. The gush of this genesis extended into more prolific and flourishing ideas, which gelled together and mirrored what I felt at any given moment in time. My words wove experiences into a canvas of word pictures, syncing and resonating with the layers of ideas embedded within my psyche.

The poems in book 'Riding the Moments' have been a unique experience, where, for continuous 21 days, I was able to curate an otherwise dispersed focus and document my multi-various emotions, diverse ideas, and deeply entrenched experiences. These poems reflect my various colors and moods—sanguine, playful, straightforward, distant, and sometimes even far-fetched or whirling within.

Armed with sensitivities and sensibilities—some common, some unique— I have tried to craft my emotions and feelings into a string of words, creating images that are often overlooked,their beauty gone amiss. Even a remote connection, however small, can trigger a magical frame where one's own memories resurface, filling the mind with a gushing stream of happiness and nostalgia.

And so, I earnestly wish for each of you to find your own spark within these pages.

The Journey

Man, God—thy holiest creation!
Sight blinded by the glint of flint;
can, but does not, sight the truth,
voice muted by the deafening sound
of the clinking gold around.

Man– won't travel to unravel,
the truth – the eternal truth,
unseeking, created in God's mould- free yet
bonded,
but not to love, compassion, or even
inclusion!

But why...? Has man broken tradition old?
While some others died to live, he now
barters his soul for gold.
Into the abyss plummets his soul–bound,
gagged, and subjugated-

                    despairing on
the fishy turrets he lies—lonely, cold, and
soulless.

The swings of Life

I and Me—together, travelled in the sun,
traversed in the rains;
In life's mazes—through darkness and light
and the patchy bowers.
                  Like a butterfly,
enamored with colour and fragrance;
                        Flitting in time and
coursing through winds, sensing flowers.
                Taming challenges, the swaying
winds and riding the waves.

 At the peak, eyes alight with dreams
realized—and more to conquer.
At the onset of evening… no fright, no
tribulations,
Ready anon, to cruise along the life river—
now at Delta; with wonder,
With zest, all might; none of confabulations.
Oblivious of the unknown yet to unfold, the
one conceived but concealed!

Now the pace slowed, direction straight;
clutching the inescapable—where no hand to
hold;
                                    the night
stealthily approached—nibbling at the
brightness;
Thickening darkness, evoking tremor-
unusually odd.
    Stars twinkle as if in mirth—meeting with
the Creator—yet, fearfulness?
For now, pathways—unstilted byways— dark,
pinched, and slimy.

                              But a little slip,
some loss... cloudburst to fill a void;
                    Void absorbs me
silently... clueless, like uncontained water in a
well.
                              From the abyss
looms a ray—my mooring; do not deride!
Nebulous yet steely, and my spirit rises like a
phoenix to ubiquitous ether.
With a pluck of courage—its cost for an
ever-effervescent life.

Rainbow... Fragrance... Valediction... on the
horizon;
With head held high, and eyes shining like
dew,
My spirit— energized ether, buoyant like
a cloud—
To chart a new course... sped with zest anew.

Learn... to be !!!

Difficulties surrounded me so I could learn
circumvention;
Confusion clouded me so I could learn,
crystallization;
Subjugation shackled me so I could break
free... into freedom;
Loneliness engulfed me so I could uncover
and learn communion;
Avarice overpowered me so I could learn to
cleanse, to shine in honesty;
Tears submerged me so I could bubble out...
to exuberance of gaiety;
Violence overpowered me so I could learn the
immensity of tranquility;
Ostentation propped me so I could traverse
the ground of simplicity...

Society of myth, make-believe, of who's who?
Competing to subserve all humanity and
even a sage,
These shackles- created, imposed to cage;

Break open now, the only one—you, to enhance
Throbbing life within, each moment till final ado;
Surge like a soulful song, no fragmented dissonance
Of dis-ease, an unease, a pained body, or a torn mind.

Thoughts in Passing...

Under the blue dome, semi-clad with plumes
of clouds,
Leaf-laden branches—in multi-hues of green
yellow—
dancing to the winds rhythm, creating a swirl
on the grass,
Are small yellow florets rooted firmly to the
green soil.

A moist, cool, green cushion-bed for one who
chooses to lie down.
Paved pathways lit by the hide and seek of the
dancing shades;
Crisp winds fondling the face, rippling the
glades;
Kids frolicking in sparkling fountain
waters—behind a war memorial!

In remembrance of martyrs, who sacrificed
life for Peace and Harmony, so rare.
For me, peace feeds life, ensconced as we are
in it—but unaware.

Only harmonious elements create and beget
life,
Now in disarray, causes catastrophes for us;
we seldom realize!

Humans - weirdly complex: crave peace in
war,
Health amidst sickness, love amidst hate, and
money when poor.
Man is rich when he can feel,
connect, and care with the source of life—
And only then can he experience exuberance
and contentment—life's wholeness!

Through the Dancing wind

 Lying on the grass— cool, moist, green— to
sight,
Swaying branches to the symphony of wind;
A clean blue dome under clouds, worn
out like muslin white.
Peering through the dancing leaves to
unwind.
Sun twinkling above as a star, unblinding to
the eye.

Airferry pathways above—now made, then
erased—as clouds
move ahead in the downturned vessel up
above, ever changing perpetually!
Clouds, like swarms of ducks, dazed
by openness, flying inebriated.
A moment, significantly insignificant, till
light fades,taken over by darkness,
Always present but ever transient,
as permanent as approaching death.

Delicate, as firm, and as uncertain as this
life-breath… it could be the last!
A deep peace within—in thoughts and
emotions;
Just me, my breath, my soulful moment—
seemingly eternal yet slipping by:
So very robust, long ferrying people through
their life…
Nature—its green cushiony lap to the blue
shroud above—all-sustaining, maternal!

AFTERTHOUGHT...after my morning walk'

The dark woods! Here I come in glee to thee.
Dark groves, creepers on trees twinning,
untwining, caressing;
Dense undergrowth—soft, dewy—yet no one
can flee.
Washed leaves shine, rays scattering around
and embracing ;
No sign of storm—howling, tearing,
testing—of yester-night;
All darkness now melted with morn's
light...now all serene, quiet.
The thick greens, flowers in all hues and
colors, fragrant and bright;
Birds chirping, squirrels scampering,
peacocks dancing in delight.
It's enchanting, so divine...an invisible soul
in a silken bind!
Can there be another heaven?... When nature
so beckons to be wined!

As the glance glides up, from the ground to
the sky,
Scantily filtered rays bio-scopically become
the sunshine.
Branches dance to the tunes of gliding winds,
a little shy.
Oh, you! Raise your thoughts from base to
sublime,
Kindled with compassion, away from fear—
of pelf and self!
For you were born free—to dream limitless
within the 'confines' ...you, an elf!
Each unique, ever-changing, like no one but
self;
Cast although in the same mould, but molten
on the life-shelf.
Life is emptying out... the invisible goalpost
near!
Hurry you must, before the race is over... but
not lost!

The Feet - up in arms with -'The Face'

The feet were all in knots,
Of the aged, and of the tiny tots.
Had been disgruntled for so long !... that they
were not getting their due care.
As the face was delicately looked after, with
undue dainty care.
Raised slogans for awareness—'Give us our
due, at least.'
Filed a case of abuse at the Head- judge's
court, feeling stifled and unappeased.

The case was rostered to be heard, each to
argue their own.
Both appeared in court gowns, to tear each
other down.
Head-judge (The) with gavel took the chair,
called for argument one on one.
Intently listening, all-sanguine before passing
verdict on who had won...

My Lord, I am sick, tired, and feel crushed
under the body's weight.
To put me up and you... down, My Lord, was
God's plan!!!...that's His fate.
Caged, suffocated I feel...covered with shoes
all day long;
Face caressed by sunlight, wind; is all
creamed, washed umpteen times.
I am the identity!!! You walk on the ground,
so are covered for safety... you face oblong!
Exposed to heat, dust, and cold,
So I am cleaned many times!
 The dead nails are polished more than my
live skin...?
 Even so, with my crowning glory...
 there we are akin!
 I carry them to the office, to home and
faraway lands,
 Yet have cracks and corn!
 ...You don't go alone, we walk as one body—
hand in hand,
Hey... so don't be forlorn!
 I am kept all socked up, perspiring in
darkness, unperfumed.

I should be scrubbed, washed, and creamed as
faces are...
So you should be! No difference there!...I
perspire in brightness, all perfumed!
All in humans' head, oh fool!!! Some take
good care.
My grouse remains, isn't the skin all over
same?
Then, why the discrimination if the body is
one... such a terrible shame!
You are right, of course!... but we are small
things in their life.

The Head-Judge (The) opined: All humans are
not the same.
Conscious though only some are, but options
they have many....
To care and comfort feet—to drive, jive and
thrive.
Bemoan I do!!! Humans exclude, rule by
discrimination...times a many.
Power they want to wield... but never yield;
So they use me, you, the body, the Nature,
even God...everything to gain in life's
battlefield!!!

Beware, humans for a happy future: YOU must learn... to Nurture!!!

Civilization in Autumn

A lone tree in a dried-out forest, bleak;
Sans greenery, color, and glory;
Naked, exposed cracks in the bark,
Leaves ready to let go; a sight quite unsavoury.
For devoid of values, man is like a cork.

A Zombie – committed to mundane;
Not a moment to spare for nature,
Nor for the plight of others around;
Man- an animal, in caricature,
overshadowed by concrete; trapped and
bound.

Old age – the turning point –
Rigid yet flexible, for want of power.
seeding thorns, aspiring for flowers;
can't break their self-made moulds, fear of
new, to start afresh.
                                        Younger
generation alien, flexibility concretized!

Nature Captivated

From a blossoming flower hung a dew drop,
Shone like a miniature sun;
On the blade of glass glistened another, like
the earth in the sun.
The shimmering ray travelled covertly
through leaves amid cascades,
Nature's music abounded—chirpings birds,
whispering wood, whistling winds—
Soulful; but to man's ear—soundless, all
unheard and wasted!

The man walked past—without a glance,
without an ear—to his mansion;
Sightless, earless...into the basement he went,
worked himself ill;
In his eve, decapacitated, isolated lying in
bed, he looked at the 'wonders' outside;
Pining to be a part of it, to connect—for
solace, for peace with self.
Alas! Wasted breaths! Lost, undiscovered,
wasted within...for gold and glitter.

Out...and Without

Standing on the hill—Dusk fading
into darkness-
       The city below throbbed, glowed
and glittered with light.
       Fair, fireworks, sparklers; sweets
exchanged hands –
       Children bubbled, the young
crackled, and the old hobbled with delight.

       Unnoticed—in the
darkest corner—a hut, where
       life struggled for life,, starved...
parched... gasping.
       emaciated life, on the ground –
streaming tears, shivering,
Convulsing, quivering; live-corpse with
parched lips; from shackles, life escaped.

       The enormous illusion—there, yet not
there—man's manifestation,
    His own web creation; surrounded yet
alone; free yet captive.

Spirit parched, body super-laden; like no
scab on dead wood! A travesty of values,
   Like water disappearing from sand and an
overt mirage in sand appears.

Maa -The Light

Breath, life's anchor,
In rhythm as the day and night;
Separate yet transfused ensconced as ethereal
arbor,
our earth in universe: in cosmos like a
street-littered with light.

It breathes, whispers, plays on the wings
of the wind,
sings, dances and reflects on the lap of the
water;
It ever germinates, rejuvenates, curates the
seeds in the mind—
Of thoughts into words and then action,
only bridled by rhythm of matter.

Pristine emotions, like words of a child,
connects a man to the heaven,
Man-made society taints, warps the child's
purity—naturalness;
Conscious not of intangible connection with
the sublime–but limitless dependence,

Mired in physicality, missing in totality the
breath's pricelessness!

The Lonely Cloud....

Seeing a lonely cloud, floating in the vast blue
sky; by it I was enamored, as others clouds
coalesced
To put a reassuring arm around it, to infuse
some solace, I ventured near.
Surprised, it looked around with its bright
countenance; now my turn to be startled!
It was silent, but its radiance shone,
exuberant with joy and copious with cheer!!

It wasn't at all desolate, nor was it lost; nor
directionless or forlorn.
No longing, not yearning; no aches, no
mourning, not even pining.
Neither did it seem neglected,
nor abandoned, nor bearing any sense of
rejection.
I, inimical— in a grey veil, so it had seemed
to me; at me now was beatifically smiling!!

Borne on the tray of golden rays, the cloud
majestically rode the wind;

Imbued with fragrance, it gently swam in
peace, oblivious to the theatre without.
Dazed, I stood—aware of the self grown
bonds and chains, of the webs around;
I, myself, limiting me, tethering my reach to
the beyond, obfuscating my prayers aloud.
And it, in its core, rejoiced in soulful notes
and dance, when it seemed alone!

My milky way

Today you arrived amidst lockdown,
like a feather—delicate and light!
Parents afraid to handle, yet in arms to
gather.
Alone...on an unknown path, they trembled
but trudged on,
The feel of you, warm to their skin; a reason
for delight!
You have grown now—from a cotton puff into
a soft silken feather.

With just your arrival, blessings showered
down,
Like a flower—delicate, fragrant and colorful
sight.
Since then, love and laughter abound like
tinkling bells—
Like cheerful chirpings of feisty birds in
boughs overgrown,
Like ducklings frolicking and nestling
in pond to delight;
Like raindrops falling on land parched—life
and aroma swell.

You are a bundle of pure joy;
The pivot of your parents world,
Giving them ecstasy and happiness.
I experienced this, almost three decades since.
Journey continues, as time flies and is looped,
Life's been bountiful, graced us with
you—your highness,
Our grandson, a prince in every regal sense.

As you grow and cross little milestones—
lispings, the very first cooing,
Sitting with support, then upright; that first
crawl on all the fours,
Each brought scintillating twinkles of joy
immense,
Like a fleet of fireflies, dancing and wooing.
Your first cutting of teeth, tiny tottering steps
brought wonderment to the fore,
A sight for delight and pride—a sure cocktail
for dance.

On your second birthday, I wish for you
endless showers of blessings and miracles:

For perennial joy, robust health, and sharp
intellect.
Also, may in your life exploration abound and
to the hilt,
With abundance and exuberance, sans any
shackles!
Traverse the chosen road, even if it is less
traveled...
Because there is only one YOU!!!

you say....

You say
I was small and tender,
No qualms, but happy to ponder—
About colors and hues,
Fragrance and trees,
Breeze and bees
Fruits and berries!
A princess on the swing,
As I came down gliding on the wind,
And went into the sky on the upswing.
In perpetual wonderment—the various
variances none existed;
Only innocence, happiness, joy, and being
fair—meant childhood.

As I grew young...thus began the race,
The innocence now yoked to brace
The grind of social situations
Inherent in the world I was born into.
The childhood ties, pure and simple,
Now masked under glint and guile—
To be seen just as the right,
Though not always righteous.

Smile bereft of genuineness
Shone, but akin to cold brass.

Now, as my hair is turning white,
I am amused, no longer trite,
At the games people played,
Without qualms, no feelings displayed.
Replacing one mask deftly with another,
Like a spy to fool foes! Do harm unto others-
Families, siblings, friends, acquaintances.
Life is gasping, even in divine largesse!
It's now an exodus... race to make-believe,
The grounding values... a laggard, so you
leave!
So lightened, you fly like a kite, wind-borne.
If the horizon darkens or winds do you harm,
Don't be lost and forlorn—come to me.

For I let the seed of life-soul germinate in
heart mine.
come to rest in the cool warmth of love and
grace,
Inebriated by the sweet nectar, drink in
happiness and peace.

Share the trove with those who yet haven't so
done!
Let soft threads intertwine into a cocoon
divine;
Spread and sprout only that which you like
and thrive.
Feed on that which nurtures and nourishes,
So in turn, let the humaneness within each
flourish.
Let the light and warmth of care and
gratitude
Glow, permeate, and create a halo across all
latitudes.

The Jungle within…!!

I went outdoors to bring fodder for animals
at home,
Unaware that I was a fodder for savages who
roam.
In this land of Ram and Buddha, isn't respect
just for name?
I was mauled, molested, subjugated, mutilated
in your land again!
Why was I born in this partisan land ? Had
no choice, am I to be blamed?
How about the families who raise such sons,
untamed?

On my pyre, let the social falsities burn, in
utter shame;
Goddess Durga, Parvati, Saraswati…
defiled all were, put to bane.
In temples to these, you pray and outside, a
girl prays for her life… in alms.
Two faced! What you say, you don't do; what
you do, no guts to admit.
Brutely you trample to break my body, but is
my spirit in tatters?

You touch to defile, then doesn't
untouchability matter?

Each one, far and near, I beseech all: if you
have grit and valour.
Cleanse yourself of caste, creed, and colour!
Like mirror, into small pieces the society been
broken,
By those in veils to hide their ogre face and
malafide intention.
This wasn't my destiny! It was plotted and
planned with progression—
When some were 'more equal' through access
to power, money and education!

The Road that turns...always turns!!!

Pushed outside, I saw the light; all lit up but not the road.
Submerged consciousness by basic needs at home shackled me.
Home opened into the playground and then into the competition at its height.
Amidst endless contemplation, I missed the road, walked the ground in virtual glee.
The road kept turning, with me unawares, life raced by.

Each turn ushered a change anew, with the mirage of the road still hidden.
The webbed chains grew stronger, me entwined by social fodder.
I saw the people who had seen the road. But in vain, I, by my ego, forbidden!
The self-sewn grid held me captive, I jostled for space in the ground... by soul's order.
The turn now occasionally visible, but the switch to the road still at large!

The urge for the forsaken road kindled-like a
rising up sapling, after rooting in the
sowed-ground;
The light hit hard; And the hidden road
appeared – as if from nowhere!
Into the oblivion, the wilderness melted; the
streak of immanence abound.
Buoyant, un-blinkered, unfettered, joyous,
I floated like a cloud everywhere!
The road on its few last turns! The same
doorway!! Circle near completion.

The road's fragrance enticed me, the voidness
in me a buoyancy loaded.
In me, each experience, every turn, found its
meaning like –
Each brick in a temple, each cell in a life, each
decibel in a sound instilled.
Me, habitual of often turns, no longer
skeptical of the straight, lit up road: a spike
I am ready to embrace the beginning ,and also
the end; which is every where!!!

My Green Brigade

Fresh morning, new life; filtered through
sunshine- golden and glorious!
My eternal friends, awaiting my arrival- to be
beside me as always.
And I, conscious at every step, of what they
generate to keep me alive;
As I pass each of all, each a canopy- a cover,
cool and copious;
Adorned with dangling dewdrops-like rings
of fire in dark-lit skies!!
Primed to cascade down into the green lap
blessed, so for life to thrive!!!

As I walk past another mate, arms out to
embrace, like boughs cool tender;
Out to caress my entirety, both to nourish
and suckle on my innermost core.
Yet I, oblivious, unwittingly partakes
partially; but not my life soul-mates !
In my absence, they are no truants. In my
company, too, equanimity-evenly fair.

Eternal friends, mates: each tree around-
standing tall- to love on me, pour!!
My Green Brigade-my savior, yours too; on its
blessing only does life resonate!!!

The Diffused Masks

As I sat before my core mirror,
Back at me, smiled my sacred self-
My core, inert inner beseeched; venerable and
inviolate.
I am peace, I am love, hope, and joy in
glimmer,
And so also in the colors of butterflies, in
sounds of sea shells,
in the fragrance of flowers, and in the winds
which with the waves resonate!
Within I am, but yet to experience the
boundless,
Hovering at the cusp of it, ethereal gossamer
through, in me expressed!!

From the enlivening stupor, I arise;
The masks everywhere appear,
Still not devoid of them- like a puppet
controlled, I feel;
Caught in the dragline of the web, life
struggles to drop disguise!
At every step countless impediments- masks I
encounter

Some without, most within; unabashedly they
cling to me with zeal.
In circles I move, reaching nowhere, but
memories everywhere!
Can see the traces of the footsteps, to follow
needs courage extraordinaire!!

The Star-lit... Dark Space !

Lying down on the cool, moist, green bed,
tranquilly gazing above,
Peering down at me, a starlit dark sky -
Bride's sequined cape, dazzling, bright-
As if to gauge earth's life-dance rhythm, in
discord, in shambles... some gaping,
Some blinking- as if awestruck by the
abundance of divine's love-fed trove!
For me the moon gently waltzing, as if tracing
its light path in delight;
All of us -girdled by the dark space-bound
together-as a tuned up watch spring!!

Wondering at the interplay- vast and
profound, Lilliputian I feel;
In a flash- a thought I am seized of –how
condescendingly looks a man
Upon all life around, also decimates, scars and
ruins to suit ego and self.

Pretermiting- one among all life- witless
himself in the same wheel!
Earning by quashing, crushing and scaring
life-elements around-a deadly clan!
My quest-can concern, care,
benevolence girdle mine, your, our space-for
all life to Heal!!

Continuously becoming into being, humanity
being the earnest end in design;
So the space is a fertile cauldron, a
concierge–all is one with no divisive line!!

The Centipede's Travels

As into the parched earth, the soft drizzle like
spray seeped,
Above on the leaves, haloed water droplets
like pearls hung;
The immersive petrichor urged a reciprocity;
a yearning for a walk!
Insensate to many ruined hearths of
unnumbered lives, now inundated;
Donning my shoes, drunk on cheer strolled
on to capture the visual feast!

Feather-touch moist wind, diverse sights in
mist-veil. My heart sprang-
the trees-gleaned, lush-green:
leaves-silver-plated platter: a dancing
peacock!!
Then centipedes, I espied on the sludge,
emerging steadily, courage unabated!
Lo... so many of them,milling around! Some
on the road meditatively trudging!
Sitting myself on the kerbside, gazed in awe
at the creature so delicate!

With deca- tiny, tender, tiddy- feet; I watch
one-rowing the road behind;
Bound in all focus, circumventing pebbles -as
if a aimful driven man lone
Navigating the vast Amazon testing his
mettle equanimous, ungrudging!
The little centipede: in its little coach frame,
its eyes miniscule, intricate;
I marveled how massive the grass, shrubs,
trees appeared & road pebbles!

As a car sped by, did it trigger any alarm,
jitters, quiver or any trepidation!
Did my footsteps spark any dread, tremor like
Dinosaur's foot poundage!
Did the horn shrill, generate ultrasonic
booms or had insentient sensibility!
Nevertheless the creepy, crawly, nymph,
centipede traversed the wide stretch;
Reverence in me welled up; so paid homage
to enormity of each life at large!!!

Basking in the Sunshine...

The rising sun, the slanting rays- dispelling
the dark-veil, ready to caress,
Disperse to cloak with a mantle-
golden-hued gossamer and diaphanous!
Animating creatures and bestowing all- life
and luminescence, in embrace.
The wind also in tandem- wafting gentle and
serene- eager to chorus!
Dance of life in jubilation, all in concert, in
harmony- a synergistic osmosis!!

Shafts of gold gleaming bright, traversing-
piercing all bridled by connoisseur:
-on the blooms, rose wrapped in a fondling
golden wrap, dew like pearls rare!
Hanging precariously, fragrance sweet and
pleasant- accentuating the air:
The golden beams- through the palms sieving,
branches swinging indolent care:
-Patting the buds :cherishing ,urging the
flowerets to blossom, a love affair!!

I, too basking in concert -peering, savoring
the beauty, luxuriant & abundant:
View delightful, invigorating, radiant like a
rainbow, multihued & flamboyant!
I, feeling stirred & evocative, blessed its
virtue-perpetual, dynamic exuberant
Accede to just being-a simple life- alive to
experience all, without complaints:
Just happy to be alive, cocooned by
life-nature, robust, resonant & jubilant !!